Joseph
and the
Dreaming
Pharaoh

To Megan

First published in Great Britain in 2017

Society for Promoting Christian Knowledge
36 Causton Street, London SW1P 4ST
www.spck.org.uk

British Library Cataloguing-in-Publication Data
A catalogue record for this book is available from the British Library

ISBN 978-0-281-07472-3

13 5 7 9 10 8 6 4 2

Typeset by Gill McLean
Printed in Great Britain by Ashford Colour Press

Produced on paper from sustainable forests

Joseph
and the
Dreaming
Pharaoh

Fiona Veitch Smith

Illustrated by
Andy Catling

Wakey Wakey

SPCK

Joseph was one of **twelve brothers** who used to live with their **dad** and **stepmothers** on a farm in the land of **Canaar**

On the farm were sheep, goats
and *lots* and **lots** of cows.
There were **fat** cows and skinny cows
and **somewhere-in-between** cows,
but **Joseph** loved them *all*.

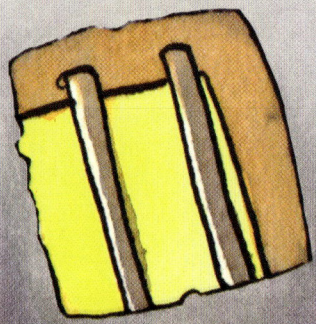

Now, Joseph no longer lived in Canaan. He lived in a **prison cell** in Egypt with only **imaginary cows** to keep him company.

How he got to be in such a **terrible** place is a long, sad tal

but it started with his **jealous brothers**
and ended with a **lying lady** and a **forgetful servant**.

Poor Joseph.
He had been **waiting so long** to be set **free**.
He prayed **every day** that **God**
would cause the **butler** or **someone** to **remember** him,
but God did not seem to **hear** him.

Joseph began to **despair**
that he would **ever** walk on **green grass**,
feel the **sun** on his back
or breathe **fresh air** again.

Joseph didn't **know** it, but **behind the scenes,** **God** was at work.

The **King of Egypt** was a man known as **Pharaoh**.

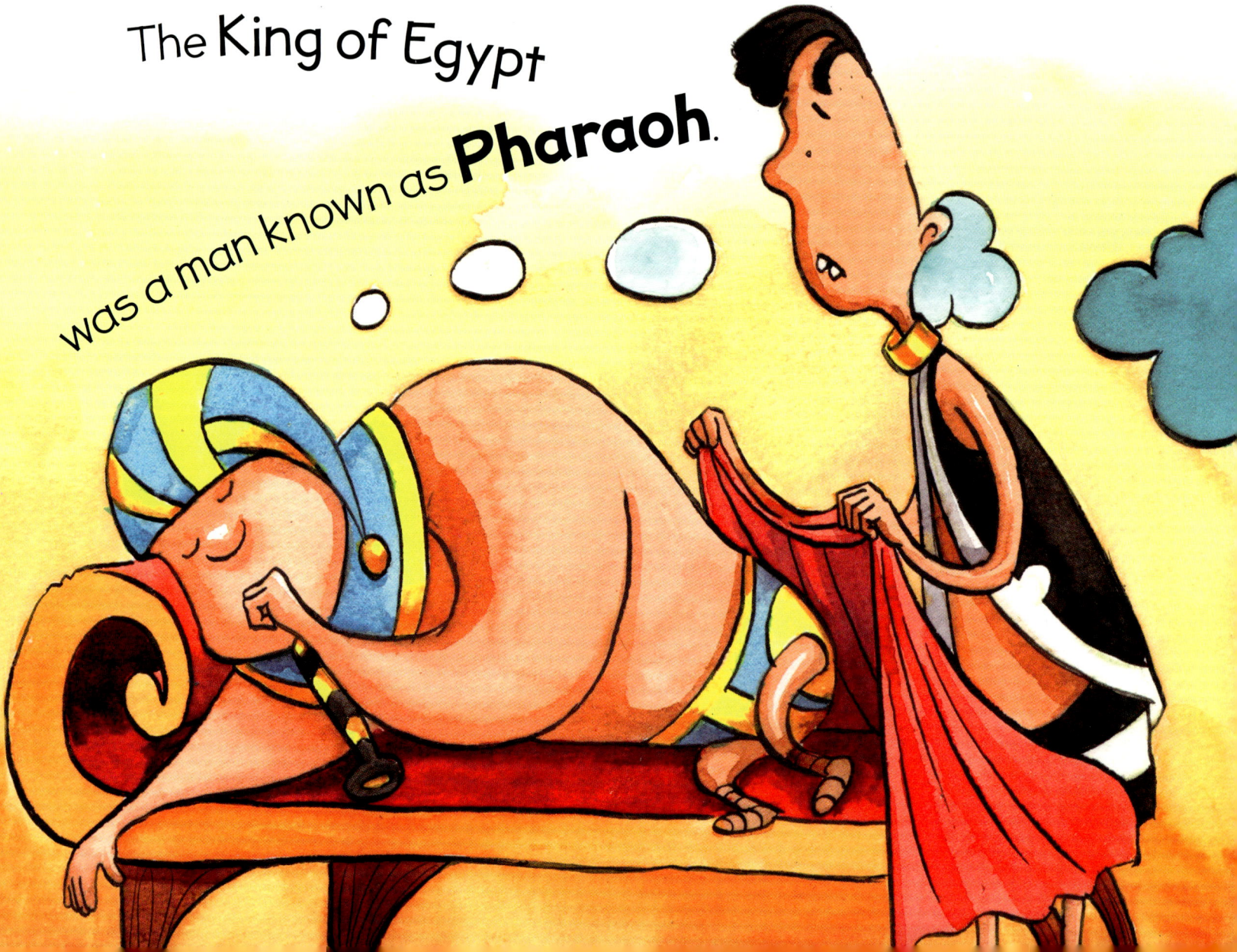

Pharaoh had not been **sleeping** well
so he was in a **very grumpy** mood.
He'd been having these funny **dreams**
and they were keeping him **awake with worry** . . .

In **one** dream, he was standing beside the **River Nile**, when out of the water came

seven **fat**, sleek, **handsome** cows.

They grazed among the reeds
and were so **happy** eating their lunch that they didn't see

what was **creeping** up behind them...

Then, coming out of the river,
were **seven skinny** cows.
They were the **scrawniest** and **ugliest**
Pharaoh had ever seen.

They crept up on the **fat** cows and,
to Pharaoh's great **surprise**,
gobbled them **all** up.

Pharaoh woke up in a **cold sweat**.
'Oh, what a ***terrible*** dream!' he thought,
but went back to sleep.
This time he saw **seven fat**, healthy
ears of **corn** growing on a **single** stalk.

'Hmmm,'
thought Pharaoh,
'that will make some
nice bread.'

He sat down and watched it, waiting for it to be **ready** to **harvest**.

Then, *another* stalk of **corn** grew up beside the first. This **too** had **seven** ears on a **single** stalk, but it was **limp** and **weak**. 'Hmmm,' thought Pharaoh, 'that will ***not*** make nice bread!'

He turned back
to watch the
healthy corn grow, but, to his **horror**,
the limp and **weak corn**
attacked the healthy corn
and **gobbled** it
all up.

Poor **Pharaoh** woke up in a **cold sweat** again, but this time he did *not* go back to sleep.

He got up and called for all the **magicians** and **wise men** of Egypt to come to the **palace** where he told them his **dreams**.

But the **magicians** were just as **puzzled** as Pharaoh. None of their **books** or **charms** or **visions** could tell them what the two dreams **meant** and, although they stayed up **all** night talking, they could not figure it out.

So Pharaoh sent them home.

Pharaoh was very **glum**.

He asked his **butler** for a goblet of wine.
As the **butler** was pouring it, he **remembered** something!
'My lord,' he said, 'Remember when you were **angry** with m[e]
and sent me to **prison**?'

Pharaoh said that he did.

'Well, there was a **young man** there called **Joseph** who knew the **meanings** of dreams. He *said* I would get out of prison and I *did*.'

Pharaoh sat bolt upright and declared,

'**Send for this Joseph!**'

So, *finally*, Joseph was **released** from prison and given a **new set of clothes**. Then he listened to the **King's** dreams.

'Tell me what they **mean**!' said Pharaoh.
'I shall have to ask **God**,'
said Joseph, who knelt down and **prayed**.
After a while, Joseph said,

'God has given me the **answer**.'

'Both dreams have the *same* meaning,' said Joseph. 'The seven **fat** cows and **healthy** ears of **corn** mean there are going to be **seven** *good* years of **harvest** for Egypt …

but they will be followed by seven ***terrible*** years of drought when there will **not be enough food** to feed ***all*** the people.'

Pharaoh was shocked.
'What should we do?' he asked Joseph.
Fortunately, Joseph was a
very **wise** young man and he said,
'You should put the **wisest** man in the
kingdom in charge. He should build
a **giant** storehouse and

I'M WISE

PICK ME

for the **next seven** years, save as *much* food as possible. Then, when the **seven** years of **drought** come, there will be **enough food** for *everyone*.'

'Well,' said **Pharaoh**, 'I can think of no one **wiser** than **you**.'

So **Joseph** – the boy *hated* by his brothers and sent to prison for something he *hadn't* done – became the **most important** person in Egypt.

With the help of his faithful **cows**, he set about saving **the people** from **starvation**. **God** really *did* have an **awesome** plan!

Also available in the Young Joseph series

Joseph and the Rainbow Robe
978-0-281-07468-6

Joseph and the Jealous Brothers
978-0-281-07469-3

Joseph and the Lying Lady
978-0-281-07470-9

Joseph and the Forgetful Servant
978-0-281-07471-6

Joseph and the Fearful Family
978-0-281-07473-0

Joseph and the Hidden Cup
978-0-281-07474-7